Filipino-American Is In The Heart (2025)

Short Poems as a Naturalized Immigrant in the United States

Erika Dani Baccay

Made with ❤ on the BookLeaf Publishing Platform
www.bookleafpub.in
www.bookleafpub.com

Dedication

To the brown brothers and sisters

Preface

I chose to move forward with this poetry book for the fact that I am an immigrant and I have words to say. No matter that both English and my native tongue does not come naturally to me but yet I still choose to represent my race and ethnicity. To show others that yes representation does matter for not only are we expressing our realities to the world but we're providing to the reader little moments where one can connect and grab and think.

Acknowledgements

I'd like to acknowledge the brown community. I'd like to acknowledge the black community. For piloting movements and creating a space where loving one's skin color is expected and trusted. Humans in general are pretty great.
I will be using the Tanaga Filipino poetry style, consisting of four lines with seven syllables each. Traditionally, in the Filipino language — however, in the essence of being an American citizen; all poems are in English.

GtG.

1.

She goes to water the plant
Wind urging the chimes to chant
He goes to sit in the sun
Mom yells, "SPF lotion!"

2.

If I can get you to smile
With a laugh that's out of style
Would you be open to me
With a mortgage and house keys

3.

I am a naturalized
Immigrant with deep black eyes
Filipino; born and raised
American; a bit dazed

4.

My child, go smell like the sun
Play with its soft rays my young
Once streetlights turn on, run home
Growing as the seed I sown

5.

Paradoxes culture and race
Assimilates to keep pace
Content, identity lost
Barely fit in at a cost

6.

Black culture helped strengthen mine
Love for love, there is no line
Their zealous made me zealous
Focus on what was precious

7.

I receive your love, humbled
A sense of duty, rumbled
Receive the gifts of the lord
For god urges us forward

8.

Skin color is identity
Harmonize with and evolve
A hue mixed with shades pretty
Anticipating resolves

9.

Smile smile smile smile smile culture
Flock of birds chirp chirp chirp chirp
nurse nurse You should be a nurse
Verse, a blessing or a verse

10.

Select willingly one's soul
Morals shaped by what was whole
Observe slowly one's values
Resonate with what you choose

11.

Parallel play but as old
You loving me pretty bold
Walking together towards
The start... lowering my guard

12.

Why do we exist, I thought
It started there, curious me
Our maker follows what's wrought
I just want to better me

13.

Trust in the process more like
It is god who's in your psyche
Those words you whisper you breathe
Your spirit your soul your seed

14.

I don't have close friends; nomad
Stories of travels; far land
Constant was my family
Sky stares back, eternity.

15.

Mother oh mother we're late
Mom let's eat here, celebrate!
Mom I love you don't leave me
Never feel to let me be

16.

Thanks for always being there
I yell you yell we all yell
Ice cream is our favorite
You're a good dad. Don't forget.

17.

I grew a pair of balloons
Inflate, now I'm fighting goons
Indebted with some interest
Protecting your home in trust

18.

On this adventure, some wise
Goes to my brother, may rise
You take care of yourself more
Know your morals at your core

19.

I look at your temperament
If you react. How you do.
To care and to pay for rent.
Still not your nurse. Still helps you.

20.

My elephant ear gave birth
A beautiful unfurling
Placed bright and moist in the dirt
I'm growing, ever changing

21.

I am a poet. Artist.
Impression of a peck. Kiss.
Your belief in me. My strength.
My creations, my wavelength.